MMMMM!
SOUP JOUMOU!

CARLINE SMOTHERS
ILLUSTRATIONS BY FUUJI TAKASHI

Dedicated to:

My parents, Marcel & Hermane Joseph. Thank you

for teaching Haiti's beauty!

I love you. -- C.S.

Illustrations copyright © 2017 Fuuji Takashi

Edited by Jeremy J. Bannerman

My mom, grandma, auntie, and I all went to the market.

"Carrots, squash, pumpkin, cabbage, onions, potatoes, pasta, and more!"

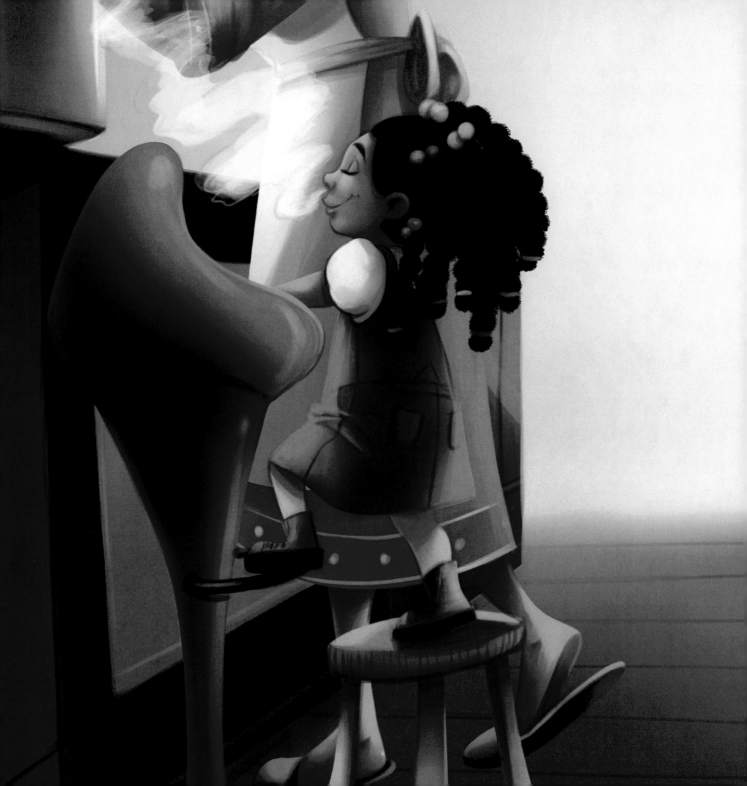

"Mmmmm! Smells so good, I could just taste it!"

In the kitchen, I watch as they laugh and share great memories of living in Haiti.

Mommy sits me down on her lap,
"Tomorrow our family will eat
Soup Joumou.

It's a Haitian pumpkin soup."

"On January 1, 1804, Haiti became the first Black Republic, after defeating the French Colonists.

We eat Soup Joumou to celebrate regaining our independence and freedom," mom said smiling.

After sitting and talking with mommy, it made me even prouder to be Haitian.

We are strong people!

That night, I had a dream about the war and how Haitians dominated.

I can't wait to celebrate with my family tomorrow!

Happy Independence Day!

Mmmmm! Soup Joumou!

Words to know...

Celebrate- a happy day or event, where people come together to enjoy.

Colonists- a person or people who moves into a new country, or settles in a new colony.

Dominated- having complete control.

French- a language or inhabitants/ citizens of France.

Haitian- inhabitants/ citizens of Haiti.

Independence– the fact or state of being independent.

Regaining- get back to.

Republic- a group with a certain equality between it's members.

Made in the USA
Middletown, DE
08 December 2022

17725932R00018